Built From Scratch

Personal Brand Blueprint

Turn Your Story Into a Brand That Pays You Back

by

Brian Turner

First Edition
2025

Copyright © 2025 Brian Turner

All rights reserved. No part of this book may be reproduced, stored in a retrieval system, or transmitted by any means, electronic, mechanical, photocopying, recording, or otherwise, without the prior written permission of the copyright owner, except by a reviewer who may quote brief passages in a review.

First Edition

ISBN: *979-8-9995161-9-0*

Built From Scratch: Personal Brand Blueprint. Turn Your Story Into a Brand That Pays You Back

This book is intended for informational purposes only. The author and publisher are not engaged in rendering legal, financial, or other professional advice. Readers should consult appropriate professionals before making any business decisions.

Table of Contents

INTRODUCTION	4
Chapter 1: You Are the Brand	7
Chapter 2: Define What You Stand On	12
Chapter 3: Structure First, Then Show Up	18
Chapter 4: Say It How You Live It	23
Chapter 5: Show Up Small, Stay Consistent	28
Chapter 6: Pick Your Platforms Strategically	33
Chapter 7: Link Before You Launch	39
Chapter 8: Sell What You've Survived	45
Chapter 9: Email Is the Asset	50
Chapter 10: Protect the Brand While You Grow	56
Chapter 11: When the Brand Becomes Bigger Than You	61
Chapter 12: Always Up, But Always You	66
Bonus Section: Tools, Templates, and Swipe Files	70

INTRODUCTION

"The brand isn't you on your best day. It's you on your realest one."

Let's get something straight:
I didn't build a personal brand because I wanted to be famous.
I built one because I was tired of being broke, burned out, and invisible.

No one was coming to save me.
The business wasn't working.
The algorithm wasn't favoring me.
The bank account wasn't forgiving me.
And my confidence? Hanging on by threads of potential.

I had a story.
I had receipts.
I just didn't have structure.
And without structure, even the best story fades.

You're not here to go viral.
You're here to build something that lasts.

Because you've lived too much, survived too much, to waste your voice on trends and tactics that don't reflect who you are.

This book is the blueprint I wish I had during the rebuild, not the hype cycle. Not the peak. The silence. The stretch where nothing was landing, but everything I posted was rooted in truth.

Whether you're launching a service, selling digital products, or just trying to figure out how to show up online without selling your soul, you don't need more fluff. You need structure.

You need systems.
You need a strategy.
You need a brand that doesn't just *look* good, it *works* when you're not looking.

And most importantly, you need a brand that pays you back.

Who This Is For

This is for the:

- Quiet grinders rebuilding their voice and visibility

- Creators done chasing likes who want income instead

- Entrepreneurs ready to turn their story into a system

- Everyday people with real receipts and no roadmap

If you've ever said:

- "I don't want to be an influencer… I just want to build something real."

- "I know I have value, I just don't know how to package it."

- "I'm tired of being told I need to do more to be seen."

Then this book is yours.

No hacks.
No hype.
Just honest steps from someone who had to learn the hard way.

Let's build your brand from scratch.
But this time, let's do it with strategy.

Always up.
— BBT

Chapter 1: You Are the Brand

"The brand isn't what you create. It's what you survived."

Let's cut through the noise:

Your personal brand is not your logo.
It's not your colors.
It's not your font or your feed.

Your brand is your alignment, the invisible thread between your story, your values, and your voice.

Most people think branding is about how you *look*.
But the most powerful brands?
They're felt and not just seen.

The Brand Starts With You

Before you post anything, before you buy a domain, plan a launch, or film a reel, you need to understand this:

You are the brand.

Not a curated version.
Not the polished, personal development version.
Not the one that's easy to digest.

Just you.
As you are.
With what you've survived.

Because people don't buy information anymore.
They buy alignment.
They buy clarity.
They buy *you*, when you're in integrity with your message.

The Myth of "Becoming" the Brand

There's a lie floating around that you need to become someone to build a brand.

Nah.

You don't need a new identity.
You need to stop hiding the one you already earned.

That's why this book doesn't start with your niche.
It starts with your narrative.

Because your story is the foundation…
Not just your highlight reel,
But the moments that broke you,
The ones that built you,
And the ones that brought you here.

The Alignment Equation

Story + Values + Voice = Alignment

Let's break it down:

- **Your Story**
  What you've lived through. What you've overcome. What brought you here?

- **Your Values**
  What you stand for. What you protect. What drives your decisions, even when nobody's watching.

- **Your Voice**
  How you show up. What tone do you carry? What truth do you speak and how?

When these three align, your brand becomes magnetic.
Not because it's loud, but because it's real.

Case Study: Pain + Pivots = Platform

There's been a shift.

People used to follow you for *what* you did.
Now they follow you for *why* you do it.

The blueprint that works now isn't built on performance.
It's built on perspective.

If you've ever:

- Gone broke and rebuilt your finances
- Burned out in one lane and found purpose in another
- Walked away from something successful because it wasn't aligned

That's not failure.
That's branding material.

That's what turns pain into positioning.
That's what makes a platform worth following.

Ask Yourself:

- What part of your story do people resonate with, even when you're not selling?
- What values guide your decisions when no one's clapping?
- How would your brand sound if you stopped filtering it for approval?

This chapter isn't meant to give you clarity.
It's meant to remind you where it already lives:
inside your own story.

You are the brand.
Everything else is just amplification.

Chapter 2: Define What You Stand On

"If you don't choose your pillars, the algorithm will choose them for you."

You can't build anything stable without something to stand on.

That's where most personal brands fall apart, they start broadcasting before they build the foundation. They try to go viral before they know what they're even here to say.

Let's fix that.

Your Brand Is Not a Niche

Here's the truth:
Your brand isn't a niche. It's a point of view.

Niches come and go.
Algorithms shift.
Platforms evolve.
But your identity, your lived experience, that doesn't move.

You don't need to "find your niche" before you start. You need to define your pillars, the 3–5 core themes you stand on.

These are the things you:

- Talk about
- Live out
- Teach through your story

And the more consistently you show up in them, the more your *real* niche will find *you*.

Pillars Make the Brand Unshakable

Your pillars keep your message focused when life gets messy.
They give your audience something to return to.
And they protect you from burning out or bending to trends that don't align.

When you post, build, or monetize, everything should come back to these.

You're not just trying to be interesting.
You're trying to be aligned.

Personal Moment

When I first tried to rebuild, I kept posting about business...

but I avoided talking about the relationship challenges, the debt, the silence.

Until I realized *that was the brand*.

That was the part people felt.
That was the truth that made the blueprint worth reading.

Common Pillars Builders Choose

You don't have to pick what's popular, pick what's real.
Here are some real-world themes that show up in builder brands:

- Faith & Mental Clarity

- Resilience & Rebuilding

- Entrepreneurship & Hustle Culture Detox

- Storytelling & Creative Ownership

- Health & Discipline

- Parenting While Building

- Financial Recovery & Real Money Talk

- Quiet Confidence & Minimalist Living

These are not *niches*.
They're values.
They're perspectives.
They're pillars.

When you define yours early, you create a brand that isn't confused or forgettable.

Your Pillars Should:

- Be rooted in what you've actually lived
- Be visible in how you move, speak, and create
- Support each other (not compete)
- Be sustainable, things you won't get tired of talking about

---

Brand Pillars Worksheet

You can find templates in the **BONUS section** at the end of the book.

Step 1 – Your Truth:

What themes show up most in your story?

Step 2 – Your Message:

What lessons do you naturally teach — even when you're not trying?

Step 3 – Your Content Lens:

What topics do you *want* to talk about consistently?

Step 4 – Your Final 3–5 Pillars:

Write them out. Then test them against your next 10 posts, products, or partnerships.

Example Pillars from My Brand

- Rebuilding After Rock Bottom
- Quiet Grinding & Long-Term Play
- Faith, Focus & Fatherhood
- Turning Story Into Structure
- Monetize Without Selling Out

Every piece of content I create filters through these. Not because I'm trying to stay "on-brand" — but because this *is* the brand.

Final Filter

When in doubt, ask:

> "If I didn't get likes for this, would I still post it?"

If the answer is yes, that's a pillar.

You don't need more topics.
You need more truth.

Pick your pillars, or the algorithm will pick them for you.

Chapter 3: Structure First, Then Show Up

"Most people post to be seen. Builders post to be understood."

You don't need more content.
You need a foundation.

Because showing up without structure doesn't build a brand. It just builds noise.

And that's the trap:
You start posting too soon.
You get one piece of content to hit.
Then you scramble to repeat it.
Now you're a content machine with no clear mission and no place to send people.

The goal isn't just to show up.
It's to have somewhere *for people to land* once you do.

Your Brand Isn't the Content. It's the Infrastructure

The content might bring people in.
But the structure is what keeps them.

Structure gives you:

- A system to plug your message into
- A way to turn traffic into trust
- A home for your brand — not just a highlight reel

Without it, everything you post disappears after 48 hours.
With it, every post can lead somewhere that matters.

Your Core Brand Stack (Minimum Viable Setup)

Let's get practical. You don't need 30 tools. You just need a quiet, effective system that backs up your voice.

Here's the minimum brand stack every builder needs:

1. Email List

Not optional. If social media disappears tomorrow, your brand survives through this.

→ Tool: ConvertKit, Beehiiv, MailerLite, or even a simple Google Form to start

2. Link-in-Bio Tool

This is your brand hub. Treat it like one.
No clutter. No confusion. Just clear, direct calls to action.

Tool: Linktree, Stan Store, Beacons, or your own web page
Include:

- Your email list sign-up

- 1–3 current offers or products

- Affiliate or tools page

- Optional: "Start Here" button

3. Website or Builder's Hub

You don't need a full site at first, but you do need *somewhere* your brand can live beyond Instagram.

Think of this as your "quiet HQ."
A place for your story, your offers, your ownership.

Tools: Notion (public page), Carrd, Framer, Squarespace

Bonus Tools (If You're Ready):

- Basic branding kit (colors, fonts, voice guide)
- Scheduling tool (Buffer, Later, Metricool)
- Airtable or Notion content system

But you don't need all of that on day one.
You need structure that *matches your capacity*.

Reminder: Don't Confuse Activity with Alignment

Just because you're posting doesn't mean you're building.
Just because you're visible doesn't mean you're clear.

**Structure protects your energy.
Structure turns noise into movement.
Structure gives your brand direction, even when life hits.**

Ask Yourself:

- Do I have one clear place to send people after they engage with me?

- Is my link-in-bio strategic, or just a menu of random things?

- If someone finds me today, can they figure out what I'm about in under 30 seconds?

Don't build more content.
Build **clarity**.

Structure first.
Then show up.

Chapter 4: Say It How You Live It

"Your voice is not a brand strategy. It's the result of everything you've survived."

Most people try to "find their voice" like it's hiding in some caption formula or tone-of-voice worksheet.

But your voice isn't something you find.
It's something you unlock.

It's the way you talk when you're not trying to impress anyone.
It's the message you repeat, even when you're not trying to make a sale.
It's the truth that stayed with you when nothing else did.

Your voice is the most valuable brand asset you have.
Not because it's perfect, but because it's real.

Authenticity Isn't Oversharing

Let's get this straight:
Being authentic doesn't mean spilling everything.

It means knowing the difference between what's *for content* and what's for *healing*.

You don't owe the internet your full backstory.
But you do owe your audience *honesty* if you want to build trust that lasts.

So here's the filter:

> "Is this something I've processed, or something I'm still bleeding from?"

If you're still bleeding, protect it.
If you've processed it and pulled the lesson out, *share it*.

Voice = Story + Energy + Delivery

Your voice isn't just what you say. It's how you say it.

Here's how to break it down:

- **Your Story** – What you've lived. What gives your message weight.

- **Your Energy** – How you show up. Calm? Direct? Poetic? Bold?

- **Your Delivery** – The format. Do you write? Speak? Joke? Teach?

When these align, your audience doesn't just hear you, they *feel* you.

Content Filters: What to Post vs. What to Protect

To stay consistent and sane, you need content filters, a personal set of boundaries that decide:

- What you share
- What you keep offline
- What you post now
- What you save for later
- What you never post at all

This keeps your brand grounded in truth, but protected by discernment.

You don't have to share everything to be real.
You just have to stop pretending.

The Most Powerful Brands Don't Perform. They Reflect

Here's the cheat code:

- If you're bold in real life, be bold in your content.

- If you're quiet and intentional, write that way too.

- If you talk with pauses, wit, or punchlines, use them.

The goal is not to imitate.
The goal is to **reflect**.

Your brand voice should feel like a natural extension of you, even if no one else ever saw it.

Example: My Own Voice Rules

Here's how I personally filter my content:

- **Never** post for sympathy

- **Never** sugarcoat the process

- **Always** prioritize story over perfection

- **Speak** like I'm talking to the version of me who almost gave up

- **Protect** anything I'm still healing from

These rules keep me honest, and free.

Ask Yourself:

- If I didn't try to impress anyone, how would I actually sound online?

- What topics drain me and which ones light me up?

- Is my current content reflecting my actual energy?

- If someone only saw one post, would they *feel* who I am?

You don't need to find your voice.
You already have it.
Now it's time to own it, and say it how you live it.

Chapter 5: Show Up Small, Stay Consistent

"You don't need a viral moment. You need a repeatable rhythm."

Most people treat content like a lottery ticket.
They're waiting for that one post to hit.
The one reel. The one quote. The one lucky break.

But real brands aren't built on *moments*.
They're built on **momentum**, small, intentional steps repeated over time.

Consistency beats creativity.
Rhythm beats reach.
Structure wins even when the algorithm doesn't.

The Quiet Content Plan

You don't need to go loud.
You just need to go **often**, with purpose.

Here's a stripped-down version of what works:

1. Carousels (Truth + Value)

Teach. Reflect. Tell stories.
These showcase your point of view.

2. Reels/Shorts (Energy + Voice)

Show your presence. Share your thoughts. Use your real tone.
These introduce your brand to new people.

3. Stories (Depth + Connection)

Document your process. Share behind the scenes. Ask questions.
These build trust and intimacy.

4. Podcast/Longform (Legacy + Ownership)

Optional, but powerful.
These create depth. A place to expand your ideas beyond the scroll.

Pick two at most to start. Then layer in more if your structure allows.

Your Story Is Your Content Bank

Most people think they need more time, more gear, or more inspiration.

What they really need is to open the vault.

Your story already holds enough content to last you a full year.
You just haven't structured it yet.

Here's how to pull from it:

- Break your story into phases: before, during, after

- Pull out moments of loss, change, clarity, and decision

- Pair each one with a lesson, mistake, or mindset shift

Now instead of guessing what to post, you're pulling from what's already real.

Batching: Your Anti-Burnout Tool

If you're posting in survival mode every day, you'll flame out fast.

Here's how to create **a week of content in a single focused session**:

1. Set a timer for 60 minutes

2. Pick one core message (pillar)

3. Draft 1 to 2 carousels, 1 short video idea, 1 story series

4. Use templates or swipe files to speed it up

5. Schedule it and walk away

That's not just time management, it's brand preservation.

Use AI... But Keep It Honest

You're not too busy. You're too scattered.
And AI can help fix that *if* you use it right.

Let it assist, not replace your voice.

Try This:

- Use ChatGPT to structure captions, outline carousels, or brainstorm headlines

- Use tools like Opus Clip or Captions AI for shortform video repurposing

- Use Google Drive, Notion, Trello, or Airtable to organize your idea bank

The point isn't to make more.
It's to make **aligned** content *faster*, so you can stay consistent without losing yourself.

Ask Yourself:

- Do I have a repeatable weekly rhythm, or am I posting in panic?

- Am I pulling from my story, or trying to chase trends I don't care about?

- What platform feels the most natural for me right now, and how can I double down there?

You don't need a perfect plan.
You need a rhythm that respects your real life, and still shows up.

Small posts. Quiet reps. Unshakable momentum.

Chapter 6: Pick Your Platforms Strategically

"Every platform has a purpose, but not every platform deserves your energy."

Here's the mistake most builders make:
They try to be everywhere and end up invisible.

Or they chase trends and end up diluted.

But if your brand is going to last, you need to be intentional with **where** you show up and **why**.

This chapter isn't about growth hacks.
It's about alignment, capacity, and choosing your lane.

Distribution ≠ Community

There are two kinds of platforms in this game:

- Distribution platforms are built for reach.
- Community platforms are built for depth.

If you're treating TikTok like a community when it's actually a distribution engine, you'll burn out trying to "engage" when you should be shipping and moving.

Likewise, if you're using email just to blast updates instead of building trust, you're leaving money on the table.

Know the difference.

Use each platform for what it's designed to do.

Let's Break It Down:

Instagram = Perception + Presence

- Good for storytelling, lifestyle content, and aesthetic.
- Use carousels and reels for POV.
- Use stories to build trust.
- Great for connecting brand *feel* to brand *function*.

Purpose: Show who you are while growing a warm audience.

TikTok = Reach + Rawness

- Fast-paced content, high discovery potential.

- Less polished, more frequent.

- Good for quick takes, raw thoughts, and behind-the-scenes content.

Purpose: Expand your visibility. Test what catches attention.

YouTube = Ownership + Longform Energy

- Ideal for building authority and evergreen content.

- High search value, especially for tutorials, series, or personal story arcs.

- Shorts help feed into full videos or products.

Purpose: Position your voice. Build depth. Scale belief.

LinkedIn = Credibility + Career Alignment

- Powerful for personal story meets professional insight.

- Great for founders, consultants, and knowledge-based offers.

- Underestimated storytelling platform.

Purpose: Elevate your authority and convert with intention.

Email = Conversion + Control

- The most overlooked platform.

- This is where income lives.

- Write like you're texting your most loyal follower.

Purpose: Deepen trust. Drive action. Own your audience.

Multi-Platform Without Burnout

You don't have to start everywhere.
You don't even need to stay everywhere.

Start with **one core** and **one supportive** platform.

Example:

- IG for brand presence

- Email for conversion

- TikTok for reach

- Notion site for direction

- YouTube for depth

- IG Stories for connection

Pick what works. Then build *around* that, not on top of it.

Watch for Platform Traps

- IG makes you care too much about aesthetics

- TikTok makes you forget your voice while chasing trends

- LinkedIn makes you talk like a robot

- YouTube makes you overthink perfection

- Email makes you think no one's listening (until they buy)

Know the platform's *game*, and don't let it play you.

Ask Yourself:

- What platform matches my real voice and energy right now?

- Where does my audience naturally live — and how do they consume?

- Am I building with depth or just chasing visibility?

You don't need a huge following.
You need a clear platform strategy that lets your brand breathe, and lets *you* stay consistent.

One voice.
One direction.
One aligned plan.

Chapter 7: Link Before You Launch

"Don't wait until the product is ready to start building the path to it."

You don't need a launch strategy.
You need a **link strategy**.

Because most people spend months building a product...
Then launch it to no one.
No audience.
No traffic.
No plan.

Monetization isn't something you flip on when the product is finished.
It's something you **build into the brand** from the beginning.

Your link is not just a tool.
It's your funnel.
It's your proof.
It's your quiet sales engine.

Serve First. Then Sell.

Before you pitch anything, your brand should be doing one thing consistently: **serving.**

Your content should:

- Solve a problem
- Shift a mindset
- Share a story

That's what builds trust.

Then when you drop a link, whether it's a freebie, product, or affiliate, people don't hesitate.

Because you didn't just show up to sell. You showed up to help.

The Minimum Link Setup

Your goal is to create a link stack that works even when you're not posting.
A structure that keeps working when you're asleep, offline, or in the rebuild.

Here's the core:

1. Link-in-Bio

This is your brand menu. Not a directory. Be intentional.

Suggested order:

- Start Here (intro or featured product)
- Free download or list sign-up
- Tools I Use page
- Store or service link
- Social or content platform

Keep it simple. Use buttons, not distractions.

2. Tools Page

This is your passive income shelf. A page that lists the actual tools you use, trust, and recommend.

It should include:

- Affiliate links
- Short descriptions of what each tool does
- Your real reason for using it

This becomes a no-pressure, high-trust source of income.

3. Tripwire or Low-Ticket Offer

Optional, but powerful. This is a small product or offer priced under $20 that turns clicks into customers.

Examples:

- Mini ebook
- Templates
- 15-minute strategy video
- Audio course

Low pressure. High intent.

Quiet Funnels Work

You don't need a webinar. You don't need countdown timers.

If someone clicks your link, they should instantly know:

- What you offer
- Why it matters
- Where to start

Let the structure do the selling.
Let the story do the persuading.
Let the product do the rest.

Why This Works Before the Launch

Most people wait to build infrastructure until after they drop the product.
By then it's too late.

Start with the link.
Even if you're only sharing a free lead magnet or an affiliate link at first.

Because that link starts doing two things immediately:

- Training your audience to click

- Giving you quiet data on what works

By the time your offer is ready, the audience already knows how to move.

Ask Yourself

- Do I have one clear link I want people to click right now?

- Is that link easy to find, navigate, and act on?

- Have I started building income streams that don't require me to post in real time?

You don't need to go viral to earn.
You just need a link that leads somewhere real.

Start there.
Quiet funnels work.

Chapter 8: Sell What You've Survived

"You don't need a perfect product. You need a real process someone else can follow."

You've been through too much to keep posting for free forever.

If you've figured something out
If you've made it through something
If you've gotten results others are still searching for

That's the offer.
That's the product.
That's the start of a business.

You don't need credentials to teach what you've lived.
You need clarity, structure, and the confidence to say, "This works because I walked it."

Start With the Lesson, Not the Launch

Before you build anything, ask this:

What did I survive that people ask me about all the time?

It might be:

- Getting out of debt
- Building a business from scratch
- Pivoting from burnout
- Healing after a breakup
- Launching something with no money
- Staying disciplined when life is chaotic

If people come to you for it
If you already lived through it
You can package it

What Should You Sell First?

Here's a simple breakdown of beginner offers, based on your story:

1. Ebook or Guide
You want to teach or explain something you've done
Keep it simple, short, and specific

2. Templates or Tools
You have a system or structure that saved you time or money
People will pay to skip the guesswork

3. Coaching or Strategy Calls
You can give someone insight in real time
Start with 1:1 and scale later

4. Apparel or Merch
You want to let your audience wear your message
Make sure it reflects your values, not just a logo

5. Digital Course or Workshop
You've got a process with multiple steps
Teach it once, record it, and refine it

6. Affiliate Tools Page
You're using products or platforms that others need
Get paid to recommend what's already working for you

Price Your Pain Properly

You don't have to overcharge. But don't undercharge out of fear.

You're not selling hours. You're selling clarity. You're saving someone else from months of confusion, isolation, or waste.

Price based on:

- The transformation it provides
- The time and energy it saves

- The value of the problem it solves

If it took you three years to figure out
And someone else can learn it in 30 pages or 30 minutes
That's valuable

You Don't Need to Be an Expert

You just need to be one step ahead of the person you're helping.

The real money isn't in being perfect. It's in being **relatable and results-driven**.

Document your process
Package your path
Put a price on the shortcut

Real Examples

You:

- Rebuilt your confidence after divorce

- Launched a brand with no investors

- Created systems for daily discipline

- Built a $10K/month agency from your laptop

- Published a book with no publisher

- Streamlined your affiliate stack for passive income

That's not random. That's content, trust, and product fuel.

Ask Yourself

- What result have I helped people get without even trying to monetize it?

- What problem do I solve that used to keep me up at night?

- What do I wish I had access to when I started?

Your survival has value.
Your story has weight.
Your process is the product.

Don't just sell what you studied.
Sell what you survived.

Chapter 9: Email Is the Asset

"If your brand lives on social, it can die on social. Build where you own."

The most overlooked part of personal branding is the most powerful:
Your email list.

It's not flashy.
It doesn't feed your dopamine.
It won't go viral.

But it's the only channel that doesn't disappear when the algorithm turns on you.

The goal is freedom.
Freedom requires ownership.
And email is the only platform you actually control.

Why Email Still Wins

- Open rates beat reach.

- No middleman between you and your audience.

- You can sell, teach, connect, and automate without guessing.

- You're not renting space. You're building it.

Social platforms are leased.
Email is owned.

Start Simple. Start Now.

You don't need to overcomplicate your setup.
Start with:

- A basic email service (ConvertKit, MailerLite, Beehiiv)

- A lead magnet (see below)

- A short automated welcome sequence

- A habit of sending at least one email per week

It's not about having a perfect funnel.
It's about having a direct line to your people.

The Free Offer That Builds the List

People don't just hand over their email for fun.
You need to offer **value up front.**

That's where your **lead magnet** comes in.
Keep it tight, clear, and connected to your message.

Options:

- Checklist

- Ebook or mini guide

- Quiz

- Templates or swipe file

- Private podcast episode or video training

- Discount or early access

What matters is that it solves a real problem your audience already feels.

The First Five Emails

You don't need a 20-email sequence. You need five good ones.

Email 1: Welcome
Thank them. Set the tone. Link the lead magnet.

Email 2: Your Story
Tell the real reason you built your brand. Invite them in.

Email 3: Teach Something
Give a quick win. No pitch. Just value.

Email 4: Share Tools or Offers
Mention one thing that's helped you. This can be an affiliate link or product.

Email 5: Ask and Connect
Encourage replies. Start the relationship.

Simple. Strategic. Sustainable.

Paid vs. Free List Strategy

You don't need a paid newsletter today
But you should know the difference.

Free list:

- Builds trust

- Nurtures audience

- Drives soft sales

- Good for affiliate and product ecosystems

Paid list:

- Offers exclusive content
- Adds recurring revenue
- Works for niche or high-value insight

Start free.
Scale when the demand and value make sense.

Ask Yourself

- If my account got deleted tomorrow, could I still talk to my audience?
- Am I sending value, or just selling?
- Is my email list growing every week, even if I don't post?

Social is loud.
Email is leverage.

You don't need a huge list.
You need a real one.
One email can outperform 10 reels… if it lands where it matters.

Build the list.
Then build everything else around it.

Chapter 10: Protect the Brand While You Grow

"Growth without boundaries is just burnout in a better outfit."

You can grow fast.
You can grow loud.
You can even grow broke.

That's why this chapter exists.
Because if you're not careful, growth will pull you out of alignment faster than failure ever could.

It starts small:

- A random opportunity that feels "off" but pays well

- A sudden spike in attention that pushes you to perform

- A partner, sponsor, or platform that wants your voice but not your values

This is how brands break.
Not from a lack of content
But from a lack of clarity when the stakes get higher

You built this from scratch
So now your job is to **protect the blueprint**

Not Every Bag Is Aligned

When money shows up, it gets harder to say no.
But you have to remember: every offer that pays you costs you something else

Ask:

- Does this dilute the message?

- Does this force me to act out of character?

- Would I say yes to this if I didn't need the money?

If the answer feels shaky, walk away.

Alignment isn't cheap, but misalignment is expensive

Three Things That Keep You Grounded

1. **Your Values**

Keep them written down.
Review them before every big yes.
If your content and decisions don't reflect them, your brand starts drifting.

2. **Your Filters**

Build a set of rules for yourself

Examples:

- Never partner with products I wouldn't use

- No interviews unless I align with their audience

- No sponsorships unless I can speak freely

- No fake urgency in my funnels

3. **Your Boundaries**

Decide how often you'll create.
Decide how accessible you are.
Decide what parts of your life are offline, no matter what.

Without boundaries, your brand will become public property.
With them, it becomes powerful on your terms.

Build with People, Not Pressure

Eventually, you'll need help. But you don't need a big team to lose control.
You just need one wrong person with no context for your values

Whether it's a VA, content editor, or business partner
Make sure they understand what you're building, and what you're not willing to sacrifice

Let people support your mission
But don't hand them your integrity

Leverage AI but Don't Let It Dilute You

AI can help you scale your systems
But it shouldn't replace your voice

Use it to:

- Batch content

- Write outlines or headlines

- Streamline admin work

- Repurpose past material

But never let it write things that sound like someone else
If you lose your voice, the brand becomes forgettable

Ask Yourself

- Would the version of me who started this be proud of the direction it's going?

- Is this opportunity in alignment — or is it just attention dressed up as growth?

- Am I still creating from a place of clarity — or am I reacting to what's working?

Growth is good.
But peace is better.

Build slow if you have to
But build solid
Protect what you're building, before it needs to be rebuilt again

Chapter 11: When the Brand Becomes Bigger Than You

"You started with a story. Now you carry a mission."

At first, it was personal.
You were just trying to share your truth.
Trying to show up with consistency
Trying to earn a little from what you survived

But then it caught on

People started quoting you
Buying from you
Telling others about you

Now your story is being shared in places you've never been
Your words are showing up on shirts, posts, presentations, even podcasts

That's when you realize
This is bigger than just content
This is culture, this is community

You Can Still Lead Without Being the Star

When the brand expands, the temptation is to center yourself in everything

But your real power is learning to **let the mission lead**

That doesn't mean disappear
It means building systems and products that move without your face always being on them

It means:

- Creating content that educates without needing your personal struggle every time

- Building offers that serve others beyond your own timeline

- Training others to carry the brand with the same voice and values

You are still the root
But the tree should grow beyond you

Expand Without Selling Out

Growth is good
But growth without discernment is dangerous

Here's how to expand with integrity:

- Create frameworks, not just personal stories

- Let your message evolve, but keep your values stable

- Say yes only to opportunities that build both audience and alignment

When people come to your brand
They should get value whether or not they know your full story

That's how legacy starts

Turn Your Story Into an Ecosystem

Start thinking in ecosystems, not just episodes or posts

Your book can become a course
Your story can become merch
Your content can become keynotes
Your pillars can become partnerships
Your voice can become licensing opportunities

This doesn't mean more work
It means **more intention with what's already working**

What you've lived can scale, if you give it a structure to do so

When Others Start Speaking for You

As your brand grows, people will interpret it
Some will get it right
Some will twist it
Some will try to copy it

Let them

Your job isn't to control every narrative
Your job is to stay consistent with yours

The brand will evolve
Your role will shift
But the foundation should stay rooted in the same truth you started with

Ask Yourself

- If I stepped away from content for 30 days, would my brand still have momentum?

- What parts of my story are ready to be turned into scalable offers?

- Am I building something that could outlast me?

You are still the brand
But now the brand is also a movement

And movements require structure
Clarity
Stewardship

Let the story stay honest
Let the mission stay centered
And let the brand become what it was always meant to be

Chapter 12: Always Up, But Always You

"The hardest part of building a brand is staying yourself while it works."

You started this with nothing but a voice.
And maybe a little fear.
You didn't know what would land.
You just knew you had something worth saying.

Now you've built something real.
People are listening.
Opportunities are showing up.
And the brand is beginning to do what it was meant to do — move without asking for permission.

But here's the trap no one talks about:

As things grow,
As money comes in,
As attention increases —
you'll feel a pull to become someone else.

Something safer.
Something shinier.
Something easier to digest.

And that's when you have to ask:
Am I still me?

Stay Grounded. Stay Dangerous.

Don't let growth strip your voice of its edge.
Don't let approval smooth out the truth.
Don't let traction turn you into a product.

Your best content won't come from strategy.
It will come from honesty.

Your most successful offers won't come from trends.
They'll come from alignment.

You don't need a new personality.
You need structure to protect your real one.

Quiet Growth Is Still Growth

You don't have to go viral.
You don't have to be seen by everyone.
You just need to be clear.
And consistent.
And committed.

The brand doesn't have to be big to be working.
It just has to be **honest and moving.**

Define Success on Your Terms

Forget the metrics for a second.

Success might mean:

- Having five buyers who actually care
- Building content that helps even one person pivot
- Earning quiet income while living on your terms
- Creating space for the version of you that never got to speak before

The outside world may never clap for that.
But your peace will.

What You're Really Building

This isn't about a business.
Or a course.
Or a feed that looks like you have it all together.

This is about ownership:

- Of your story
- Of your voice
- Of your future

Your brand is the proof that you didn't fold.
That you didn't water yourself down to fit in.

That you turned survival into structure.
And clarity into movement.

Ask Yourself

- Am I building something I'll be proud of in five years?

- Do I still sound like me?

- Have I built a brand that gives me freedom, or one that quietly controls me?

The name of this chapter isn't just a phrase.
It's a reminder.

Always up
That means no matter how slow the climb,
no matter how quiet the season,
no matter how many pivots or pauses —
you never stopped moving.

More importantly:

Always you.

Because your voice is the foundation.
And no brand is worth building if it costs you that.

Bonus Section: Tools, Templates, and Swipe Files

"Clarity is power. Structure is freedom. Use both."

You've done the inner work.
You've learned how to build the foundation, the platform, and the income.
Now it's time to lock it all in with tools that keep you moving.

This section includes swipe files, templates, and visual layouts. Not to replace your voice, but to support it.

Use them. Tweak them. Own them.

---

1. Caption Starters

Use these to simplify your writing process and stay aligned with your brand pillars.

- "This didn't go viral, but it changed everything for me."

- "Before I figured this out, I was stuck for months…"

- "Here's how I rebuilt without going broke or losing my mind."

- "If you're starting from scratch, save this."

- "What I thought would break me ended up teaching me this…"

2. DM Templates

Use these to reach out or reply with clarity and confidence.

Affiliate product collab pitch:

> "Hey [Name], I've been using [Product] for [real reason]. I'm building a tools page that features things I trust, not hype. Would love to chat if you're open to a quiet collab."

Guest appearance or interview pitch:

> "I'm building a brand around rebuilding, no fluff, no filters. Would love to join your platform for a real conversation if it aligns."

3. Email Templates

Lead magnet delivery (Email 1):
Subject: Here's what I promised

> Hey [Name],
> As promised — here's your [name of freebie].
> I don't do spam. Just real stories, tools, and proof.
> Let me know if this helps. I read every reply.

Story email (Email 2):
Subject: The turning point

> I almost quit.
> Not once. Several times.
> But one shift changed everything for me: [insert lesson]
> That became the foundation for [product/pillar/platform]
> You don't need a breakthrough. You need a repeatable step.
> Let me show you.

---

4. Builder's Tools Page (Layout Sketch)

Title: Tools I Actually Use

> No fluff. Just the platforms, apps, and systems I use to run my brand.

- Link-in-Bio: https://linktr.ee/brianbturner

- Voiceover Tool: https://try.elevenlabs.io/qobsuq525qs6

- Online Store: https://bbtapparel.com

- Ebooks & Docs: https://amzn.to/47HADMQ

Visual Tip: Keep this clean. One image, one tool per row.
Link Placement: Add this on your Linktree or website navigation bar.

---

5. Linktree Layout (Minimalist Version)

1. Start Here (Intro or featured product)

2. Free Download (Lead magnet)

3. Tools I Use (Affiliate stack)

4. Work With Me / Book / Course

5. Join the List (Email sign-up)

Tip: Only show what you're actively promoting.

6. Brand Pillars Worksheet

Step 1: Your Truth
What themes keep showing up in your life and story?

Step 2: Your Message
What do people naturally ask you about?

Step 3: Content Lens
What topics energize you — even if they don't perform?

Step 4: Final 3–5 Pillars
Sharp, honest, aligned. These shape every decision going forward.

---

7. Reflection Prompts

Use these when you feel stuck or off-track.

- What part of my brand still feels performative?

- What content do I keep avoiding — and why?

- Am I chasing growth or building structure?

- If I had to rebuild tomorrow, what would I protect first?

- What does success look like *to me*, not to the world?

That's it.

No more waiting. No more guessing.
Start small. Stay consistent. Build from what's already real.

Always up. Always you.

www.ingramcontent.com/pod-product-compliance
Lightning Source LLC
Chambersburg PA
CBHW062121080426
42734CB00012B/2939